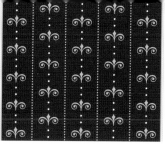

Classic Recipes of
ROME

Classic Recipes of ROME

TRADITIONAL FOOD AND COOKING
IN 25 AUTHENTIC DISHES

VALENTINA HARRIS

LORENZ BOOKS

This edition is published by Lorenz Books,
an imprint of Anness Publishing Ltd,
108 Great Russell Street,
London WC1B 3NA
info@anness.com
www.annesspublishing.com
twitter: @Anness_Books

© Anness Publishing Limited 2016

Publisher: Joanna Lorenz
Editor: Helen Sudell
Designer: Nigel Partridge
Recipe Photography: Martin Brigdale
Food Stylist: Valentina Harris
Production Controller: Pirong Wang

If you like the images in this book and
would like to investigate using them for
publishing, promotions or advertising,
please visit our website
www.practicalpictures.com for more
information.

All rights reserved. No part of this
publication may be reproduced, stored in a
retrieval system, or transmitted in any way
or by any means, electronic, mechanical,
photocopying, recording or otherwise,
without the prior written permission of the
copyright holder.

A CIP catalogue record for this book is
available from the British Library

PUBLISHER'S NOTE

Although the advice and information in this
book are believed to be accurate and true
at the time of going to press, neither the
authors nor the publisher can accept any
legal responsibility or liability for any errors
or omissions that may have been made nor
for any inaccuracies nor for any loss, harm
or injury that comes about from following
instructions or advice in this book.

PUBLISHER'S ACKNOWLEDGMENTS

The Publisher would like to thank the
following agencies for the use of their
images. Istock p 6, p11t. Alamy p8tl, p10tl,
p11b

Previously published as part of a larger
volume *The Food and Cooking of Rome
and Naples*.

COOK'S NOTES

Bracketed terms are intended for American
readers. For all recipes, quantities are given
in both metric and imperial measures and,
where appropriate, in standard cups and
spoons. Follow one set of measures, but
not a mixture, because they are not
interchangeable.

Standard spoon and cup measures are
level. 1 tsp = 5ml, 1 tbsp = 15ml, 1 cup =
250ml/8fl oz. Australian standard
tablespoons are 20ml. Australian readers
should use 3 tsp in place of 1 tbsp for
measuring small quantities.

American pints are 16fl oz/2 cups.
American readers should use 20fl oz/
2.5 cups in place of 1 pint when measuring
liquids.

Electric oven temperatures in this book are
for conventional ovens. When using a fan
oven, the temperature will probably need to
be reduced by about 10–20°C/20–40°F.
Since ovens vary, check the manufacturer's
instruction book for guidance.

The nutritional analysis given for each
recipe is calculated per portion (i.e. serving
or item), unless otherwise stated. If the
recipe gives a range, such as Serves 4–6,
then the nutritional analysis will be for the
smaller portion size, i.e. 6 servings. The
analysis does not include garnishes or
optional ingredients, such as salt added
to taste.

Medium (US large) eggs are used unless
otherwise stated.

Contents

Introduction

The heart of Italy has a vibrant history that dates as far back as the Bronze Age. From the legend of Romulus and Remus to the spread of the Roman Empire, the story of central Italy, with Rome at its core, is universally known. The influence of this glorious city was felt not only in the surrounding area of what is now Italy, but also far and wide across the world. After the decline of the empire, the region was controlled by various nations, which led to many new dishes and ingredients being incorporated into the local cuisine. These influences can still be seen today in kitchens and restaurants across Rome.

Left: The colosseum soars above the distinctive architecture in the heart of Rome.

Roman Cuisine

To many people outside of Italy, 'Italian cuisine' means dishes based on the food of Naples, whose ambitious migrants travelled the world taking the style of food they loved with them. However, there is much more to the central region of Italy, including Rome's famous gutsy pastas. Fish, too is an integral part of Roman cuisine, and features most frequently in Rome as salt cod – *baccalà*. Offal is also key, and although it has been ousted from many of the more refined city-centre restaurants, it still appears on the menus of more traditional eateries, especially those in the Testaccio area.

More conventional meat dishes include *abbacchio* (milk-fed lamb roasted to melting tenderness with rosemary, sage and garlic), *scottadito* (grilled lamb chops eaten with the fingers) and *saltimbocca alla romana* (thin slices of veal cooked with a thin slice of prosciutto, mozzarella cheese and sage on top).

No description of the vibrant gastronomy of Rome would be complete without a mention of the city's countless bars, cafés and restaurants, where Romans can be found morning, noon and night, sipping their daily cappuccinos, or eating and drinking with family and friends.

Roman Pasta

Although all sorts of pasta shapes are served in Roman restaurants, spaghetti and the local specialities *bucatini* or

Left: Salt cod features in many fish dishes across Rome.

Above: Enjoying a drink at the café on Via della Pace.

tannarelli are the favourite shapes. These chunky strips of pasta stand up well to the robust, rich sauces the Romans prefer, such as a very simple, strong-tasting *aglio e olio* (garlic and oil), *cacio a pepe* (Pecorino cheese and black pepper), *alla carbonara* (with beaten eggs. pan-fried bacon, and Pecorino or Parmesan cheese), and *alle vongole* (with fresh baby clams).

Right: Anchovies are used to add flavour to sauces.

Roman Festivals

Italians love an excuse for a party, and from the large religious city celebrations to the smaller, district festivals, they are all well worth a visit.

Festa di San Giuseppe
Though not an official public holiday, the feast of St Joseph, on 19th March, remains popular. In the run up to the feast, the deep-fried batter-balls called *Bignè di San Giuseppe* are piled high in the city's pasticcerie.

Below: The moreish Bignè di San Giuseppe.

Settimana Santa & Pasqua
The Holy Week running up to Easter is especially popular in Rome where pilgrims flood into St Peter's Square, Vatican City. On Pasquetta (Easter Monday), tradition coaxes Romans outside the city gates to feast on lavish picnics of *torta pasqualina* (cheesy bread, with salami and hard-boiled eggs) and *fave e pecorino* (raw broad beans and a hunk of cheese).

Natale di Roma
No all cities celebrate their own birthday, but Rome, 'born' in 753BC, is no ordinary city. The bulk of the celebrations take place at the Campidoglio (Capitoline Hill). The city hall and other palazzi on the hill are illuminated and fireworks are set off across the city.

Festa di San Giovanni
In the San Giovanni district, locals observe this saint's day on the 23rd June by dining on *lumache in umido* (stewed snails) and *porchetta* (roast suckling pig). The main religious

Above: Romans enjoying the Easter Monday picnic.

highlight is a candlelit procession, led by the Pope, to San Giovanni in Laterano, the cathedral church of Rome.

Santi Pietro e Paolo
The founders of the Catholic church, St Peter and St Paul are the twin patron saints of Rome, and each is honoured in his own basilica on 29th June. At St Peter's a solemn mass is conducted, whereas the celebrations at San Paolo Fuori

le Mura are focused outside the church with an all-night street fair on via Ostiense.

Festa della Madonna della Neve

On 5th August 352, there was an unseasonal snowfall on the Esquiline Hill, an event that is still remembered at the basilica of Santa Maria Maggiore. There is a special mass which culminates in a blizzard of rose petals that flutter down from the roof onto the crowds below.

Below: La Befana arrives in the Piazza Navona to give out sweets.

Christmas

In the days running up to Christmas, extravagant cribs are set up around the city and other decorations glow alongside stalls selling sweets, roasted chestnuts, sugared apples, and liquorice. Christmas day itself is a gluttonous affair with locals feasting on *fritti* (deep-fried vegetables or fish), followed by *torrone* (slabs of nutty nougat) and a sweet liqueur. The typical Christmas cake in Rome is *Pangiallo*, a delicious baked mixture of dried fruit, honey and candied citron.

Above: The basilica of Santa Maria Maggiore.

Epifania – La Befana

From mid-December, the Piazza Navona Christmas market takes place in this spectacular square, and runs right through to Twelfth Night, when La Befana, the Christmas witch, calls to bring presents to the children. As the pagan legend goes, on the day of Epiphany 'Mother Christmas' brought presents to good children only; the unfortunate 'naughty' ones found their shoes filled with coal.

Classic Ingredients

In the central region of Italy, the bustling city of Rome not only has a fascinating history, but a wonderful cuisine has developed, based on the fresh ingredients that thrive here: tomatoes, artichokes, lemons and durum wheat from the fields, sheep's cheese and meat from the hillsides, and fresh fish and shellfish from the sea.

Vegetables

The fertile soil and benign climate of central Italy makes it an ideal spot to grow all kinds of vegetables. So many savoury dishes from Rome include

Below: Pecorino cheese is similar to Parmesan.

tomatoes that it would almost be quicker to list those that do not. Artichokes are enormously popular in Italy and they are especially prized in Rome. They are flattened and fried twice for the simple but tasty dish, *carciofi alla Giudia* (artichokes Jewish style), an ancient recipe that originates from the Roman ghetto. Another much-loved dish is *carciofi alla Romana* (artichokes stuffed with mint, lemon and garlic).

Local farmers and gardeners grow all kinds of other delicious vegetables including courgettes/zucchini, lentils, potatoes, cannelini beans, broad/fava beans, peppers, and aubergines/eggplants. Aubergines crop up mainly in salads and other side dishes.

Dairy Produce

Beautiful fragrant soft cheeses abound in central Italy, and are used in many recipes, either as a topping or melted into a sauce. Mozzarella di bufala campana, or buffalo mozzarella, is the most celebrated and highly prized of mozzarella cheeses. Similar cheeses include scamorza (a kind of smoked mozzarella from cow's milk), mateca, provatura and burrino.

A harder, sharper-tasting cheese made from sheep's milk is known as Pecorino. This tasty, strong cheese can be used in a similar way to the better-known Parmesan, sprinkled on top of pasta dishes or soups.

Soft cheeses such as ricotta and cream cheese also feature in many recipes such as calzone, a folded pizza where the soft cheese is spread over the dough before the other topping ingredients. A firm ricotta is sometimes used as part of a *fritto misto*, an Italian kind of fry-up based on mixed fish and shellfish, vegetables and small chunks of cheese fried in batter. Fritto misto is often served as part of a celebratory meal.

Right: Romans love fresh artichokes and have devised many dishes that feature them.

Above: Salami is a favourite antipasti ingredient.

Meat and Poultry

Roman cuisine does not rely to a great extent on fresh meat. Chicken is perhaps the most common meat, and every bit of the bird is used, whether it's in

Below: Olives and olive oil are essential to Italian cooking.

the form of a roast dinner or a soup from the carcass. The same thrifty attitude prevails in other meat recipes. Romans are keen on offal and turn it into many dishes. Preserved pork such as prosciutto (air-dried ham), pancetta (salted, spiced bacon) or sausage is still used today as it was in years gone by when cooks eked out supplies in winter.

Pasta

Some of Italy's best-known pasta dishes originated from Rome. The Romans' passion for pasta is legendary and they take credit for inventing *spaghetti alla puttanesca* ('streetwalker's spaghetti', so named for the local prostitutes who were said to enjoy its nourishing qualities), and *spaghetti alla carbonara*, made with chopped pieces of bacon, eggs, butter and cheese.

Olives, Herbs and Spices

Olives crop up in a variety of recipes across Italy and Roman cuisine is no different in this

Above: Garlic features in many savoury Italian meals.

respect. Whole olives are used for pasta and pizza toppings and sprinkled into a salad, while olive oil is used in almost every savoury recipe as the cooking oil of choice. Fragrant olive oil can also be found as the main ingredient in the most basic pasta dressing of all, *aglio e olio* (garlic and olive oil). Butter is reserved for frying fish or blending into cakes or pastries.

A single garlic clove helps release the savoury taste of many a tomato-based sauce, but this pungent bulb comes into its own in such dishes as the above mentioned aglio el olio, as well as in lamb recipes,

Above: Capers are pungent and add a sharp tang to dishes.

where its strong flavour stands up to the equally strong taste of anchovies and vinegar in Roman roast lamb.

The local herbs are the fragrantly scented basil, which

Below: Juniper berries and thyme flavour soups and stews.

blends so well with tomatoes, as well as sage, parsley and oregano. Juniper berries bring their sharp, distinctive flavour to braised dishes such as a hearty chicken stew, while capers brighten a side dish based on yellow (bell) peppers, or the fiery pasta sauce, puttanesca.

Sweet Things
There are many wonderfully creamy, light recipes for desserts that round off a good meal. Many of them are based on cream cheese, crystallized fruit and nuts, spiced with cinnamon or vanilla. *Tiramisu*, which means 'pick me up', may not have originated in Rome, but it is an adopted speciality of the city. The ingredients – sugar, mascarpone, eggs, and espresso coffee – result in an absolutely scrumptious cold dessert.

Rome is also famous for the deliciously light fried choux pastry buns, filled with cream cheese or custard. These are traditionally prepared on Father's Day, which in Italy falls on 19th March, St Joseph's Day.

Above: The Lazio region is famous for its white wines.

Drinks
Wine is a part of daily life in Rome as it is in most other cities and regions of this grape-growing country, and a glass of wine is added to many hearty meat stews and tasty pasta sauces. Local Roman wines come from the vineyards of Lazio where the volcanic hills provide an excellent base for viticulture thanks to the fertile and well-drained land, rich in potassium. The region's reputation is mainly based on its white wines, with three particular wines standing out: Frascati, Castelli Romani and Est! Est!! Est!!! di Montefiascone.

A Taste of Rome

The best Italian cuisine is always based on the freshest possible local produce and Roman chefs focus on using the best-quality basic ingredients in their cooking. From hearty main courses such as Bucatini with Amatriciana Sauce, Roman Roast Lamb and Squid Risotto, to vibrant vegetable sides like Yellow Peppers with Capers, and Aubergines with Tomato and Mozzarella, the food and cooking of Rome is a riot of flavour and invention. This essential collection of recipes offer a lively introduction to an exciting cuisine.

Left: Fresh basil and oregano are a speciality of Roman cuisine, flavouring many soups, stews and salads.

Vegetable Soup with Semolina
Minestra alla Viterbese

Serves 4

1 large, very ripe tomato
1 large courgette/zucchini, sliced into
   thin matchstick strips
1 large onion, sliced into rings
1 large garlic clove, finely chopped
1 large celery stick, finely chopped
1 large potato, grated
1 large carrot, grated
8 parsley sprigs, finely chopped
9 fresh basil leaves, finely chopped
50g/2oz/⅓ cup semolina
25g/1oz/2 tbsp unsalted butter,
   plus extra to serve
50g/2oz/⅔ cup freshly grated
   Parmesan cheese, plus extra
   to serve

This is a typical country summertime soup, prepared when all the vegetables are at their peak of luscious ripeness. This recipe is from the town of Viterbo, which has quite a few culinary specialities that have passed the test of time.

1 Plunge the tomato into boiling water for 30 seconds, then refresh in cold water. Remove the skin and seeds, and chop the flesh.

2 Put tomato, courgette, onion, garlic, celery, potato, carrot and herbs into a large pan. Add 1.2 litres/2 pints/5 cups cold water. Bring to the boil, cover and simmer for 15 minutes.

3 Trickle the semolina into the simmering soup in a very fine stream, stirring constantly. Simmer the soup for a further 15 minutes, stirring occasionally.

4 Remove from the heat and stir in the butter and the cheese. Allow to cool slightly before serving with extra Parmesan and butter on top.

Rice and Broad Bean Soup
Minestra di Riso e Fave

Serves 4

50g/2oz/¼ cup lard or white
     cooking fat
1 large onion
1kg/2¼lb (unshelled weight) fresh
     broad/fava beans, shelled and
     skinned
30ml/2 tbsp tomato purée/paste
300ml/½ pint/1¼ cups hot water
200g/7oz/1 cup short grain rice
25g/1oz unsalted butter
1 litre/1¾ pints/4 cups boiling water
sea salt and ground black pepper
115g/4oz/1¼ cups freshly grated
     Pecorino cheese, to serve

*One of the most perfect
flavour combinations in the
world has got to be fresh,
tender broad beans coupled
with soft and crumbly,
incredibly strong-tasting
Pecorino cheese.*

1 Chop the lard and the onion together to make a blended mass (this is called battuto in Italian). Fry this slowly in a large pan until the onion is soft. Add the beans.

2 Stir the tomato purée into the hot water and pour into the pan, then season with salt and pepper. Stir and simmer for 10 minutes.

3 Stir the rice into the soup, then add the butter and stir again.

4 Gradually add the boiling water, stirring constantly and keeping it at a slow rolling boil.

5 Cook for about 15 minutes, until the rice is tender. Season and serve with grated Pecorino.

Roman Egg and Cheese Soup
La Stracciatella alla Romana

1 Put the eggs in a bowl and whisk until blended, then add the Parmesan cheese and season the mixture with salt and ground black pepper. Stir in the nutmeg or lemon rind.

2 About 10 minutes before you want to serve the soup, bring the stock to the boil.

3 As soon as it boils, take it off the heat. Pour in the egg mixture, whisking for 3 minutes, until the eggs have cooked enough to hold their irregularly shaped strands floating in the broth.

4 Ladle into soup bowls and serve immediately, sprinkled with chopped flat leaf parsley.

Serves 6
6 eggs
75g/3oz/1 cup freshly grated
   Parmesan cheese
freshly grated nutmeg or grated
   lemon rind, to taste
1.5 litres/2½ pints/6¼ cups rich,
   clear chicken stock
sea salt and ground black pepper
fresh flat leaf parsley, finely chopped,
   to garnish

This light soup is more difficult to make than it would first appear. The skill lies in making sure the delicate strands of beaten egg and cheese separate and disperse into the hot soup, rather than forming one or several large, unsightly lumps. Make the soup with a richly flavoured, clear chicken stock and ensure it is really hot, and that you pour in the egg mixture gently and with constant whisking. This is intended to be the best first course of a long Roman feast.

Deep-fried Mozzarella Sandwiches
Mozzarella in Carrozza

Serves 4

8 slices white bread, crusts removed
7.5ml/1½ tsp anchovy paste
250g/9oz mozzarella, cut into
    8 thick slices
3 eggs, beaten
sunflower oil, for deep-frying
ground black pepper

1 Trim the bread to slightly larger than the mozzarella slices. Lay four slices of bread on a board and spread each one with anchovy paste. Cover the anchovy paste with two slices of mozzarella. Season with black pepper, and cover with the other slices of bread. Squash these sandwiches together very firmly.

2 Put the beaten eggs into a shallow bowl. Slide the sandwiches into the eggs and leave to soak for 15 minutes.

3 Meanwhile, pour enough sunflower oil into a wide, deep frying pan to a depth of about 7.5cm/3in. Heat until a small cube of bread, dropped into the oil, sizzles instantly.

4 Fry the four sandwiches in the hot oil until crisp and golden on both sides, remove with a metal spatula and drain thoroughly on kitchen paper. Serve piping hot.

The word carrozza *means carriage, and these deep-fried sandwiches are the perfect vessel to carry luxurious mozzarella. It makes a delicious filling snack.*

Cheese Skewers with Anchovy Sauce Spiedini di Provatura

1 Soak four wooden skewers in water for 30 minutes. Cut the cheese and bread into equal-sized pieces about 2cm/¾in thick.

2 Thread the cheese and bread alternately on to the skewers, making sure that they are packed together as tightly as possible.

3 Cook the skewers on a barbecue or under a grill or broiler until the cheese is just running and the bread is crisp.

4 Meanwhile, put the butter and anchovies into a small pan and warm over a low heat (you can do this on a corner of the barbecue), stirring constantly until the anchovies have been reduced to a smooth cream.

5 Stir in the milk as the mixture begins to amalgamate. Season with black pepper.

6 Arrange the skewers on a serving platter, cover with the anchovy sauce and serve hot.

Serves 4

300g/11oz provatura or scamorza cheese
1 small loaf of crusty bread or sliced white bread
150g/5oz/10 tbsp unsalted butter
2 large salted anchovies, boned, rinsed and patted dry on kitchen paper
30ml/2 tbsp milk
ground black pepper

Provatura is basically a Roman version of mozzarella. It tends to be slightly more solid and less creamy than mozzarella. If you can't get hold of it, use scamorza (matured and sometimes smoked mozzarella) or fresh mozzarella that has been allowed to harden slightly over three or four days. In fact, this is a useful recipe for using up mozzarella that is past its best. It's perfect cooked over a barbecue, but can be cooked under a grill or broiler too. You could offer the anchovy sauce separately, if you prefer.

Roman Cheese and Ham Fritters
Panzerotti alla Romana

1 Mix the cubed cheese with the prosciutto, Parmesan cheese and the beaten whole egg. Season with a little salt and ground black pepper, and set aside until required.

2 Put the flour in a mound on the work surface. Plunge your fist into the centre to make a hollow. Put a pinch of salt, the butter and the egg yolks into the hollow. Blend together with your fingertips, adding 30–45ml/2–3 tbsp cold water, if necessary.

3 When you have achieved a smooth ball of dough, roll it out as thinly as possible.

4 Use a 5cm/2in pastry or a cookie cutter or inverted tumbler to cut out circles of dough.

5 Put a spoonful of the cheese mixture on to each circle and fold in half. Brush the edges with a little beaten egg white, and seal the panzerotti closed.

6 Heat the oil for deep-frying in a deep pan until a small piece of the pastry, dropped into the oil, sizzles instantly. Fry the panzerotti for 5 minutes, or until golden brown and puffy.

7 Drain on kitchen paper and serve hot.

Probably one of the earliest recipes from the culinary history of the great city of Rome, these rich and savoury dough fritters would traditionally be served as an antipasto or a snack; at some time in their history they were probably cooked as street food and sold from sizzling cauldrons of boiling oil to hungry passers-by.

Serves 4

115g/4oz/1 cup finely cubed Gruyère cheese
75g/3oz/¾ cup chopped prosciutto crudo
25ml/1½ tbsp freshly grated Parmesan cheese
1 egg, beaten, plus 2 egg yolks, and 1 egg white, lightly beaten until frothy
300g/11oz/2⅔ cups plain/ all-purpose flour
50g/2oz/¼ cup unsalted butter, cubed
sunflower oil, for deep-frying
sea salt and ground black pepper

Spaghetti with Oil and Garlic
Spaghetti Ajo e Ojo

Serves 4

400g/14oz spaghetti or spaghettini

175ml/6fl oz/¾ cup extra virgin olive oil

3 garlic cloves, crushed

30ml/2 tbsp chopped fresh flat leaf parsley

sea salt and ground black pepper

1 Bring a large pan of lightly salted water to a rolling boil. Add the pasta and stir. Return to the boil and cook the pasta according to the pack instructions until al dente.

2 Meanwhile, heat the oil and garlic together until the garlic turns black. Discard the garlic and keep the oil hot. Timing is crucial, as the oil must not burn, although it must be hot.

3 Drain the cooked pasta and return it to the hot pan. Pour over the flavoured oil and mix together to thoroughly coat the pasta in the oil.

4 Season the pasta with plenty of ground black pepper and mix in the chopped parsley. Transfer to a warmed serving platter and serve immediately.

Lots of versions of this classic Roman recipe exist, but this is a traditional one. It is reputedly very good for preventing a hangover when consumed last thing at night. Another version, Ajo Ojo e Peperoncino, includes chilli, making it quite fiery.

Rigatoni with Tomato and Ricotta
Rigatoni al Pomodoro e Ricotta

Serves 6

45ml/3 tbsp extra virgin olive oil
3 garlic cloves, chopped
900g/2lb canned Italian plum
   tomatoes, chopped and
   juice reserved
450g/1lb rigatoni
250g/9oz ricotta cheese
30ml/2 tbsp torn fresh basil
45ml/3 tbsp freshly grated Parmesan
   cheese
sea salt and ground black pepper

1 Pour the oil into a medium pan. Add the garlic and heat for about 3 minutes, or until it is just translucent.

2 Add the tomatoes and their juice, and simmer over a low heat for about 30 minutes, or until the liquid has evaporated.

3 Bring a large pan of lightly salted water to a rolling boil. Add the pasta and stir. Return to the boil and cook according to the pack instructions until al dente.

4 Meanwhile, put the ricotta cheese into a heatproof bowl and crumble it with a fork. Set the bowl in a pan of hot water and leave to heat the cheese.

5 Add the basil to the tomato sauce and season with salt and pepper. Stir. Drain the pasta and transfer it to a warm serving bowl.

6 Add the tomato sauce and half the ricotta cheese. Toss gently. Cover with the remaining ricotta, sprinkle with Parmesan, and serve.

With its broad shape and fine ridges, rigatoni is the perfect pasta to suit this particular sauce of clingy ricotta cheese and tomato. It is a superbly simple dish, but very filling and satisfying – a real family favourite for many Italians.

Pasta Carbonara
Pasta alla Carbonara

1 Bring a large pan of lightly salted water to a rolling boil. Add the pasta and stir. Return to the boil and cook according to the pack instructions until al dente.

2 While the pasta is cooking, dry-fry the pancetta, guanciale or bacon in a very hot frying pan until crisp and the fat has run freely.

3 Beat the eggs in a bowl with the cheese and plenty of freshly ground black pepper.

4 When the pasta is cooked, drain it and return it to the pan, then turn off the heat.

5 Immediately pour the egg mixture and the pancetta into the pasta, and stir everything together so that the eggs scramble very lightly and bring the other ingredients together. The fat from the pancetta should sizzle as it mingles with the pasta.

6 Serve sprinkled with cheese and black pepper.

Serves 4

400g/14oz bucatini or spaghetti
200g/7oz pancetta, guanciale
 or best-quality streaky/fatty
 bacon, cubed
3 eggs, beaten
75ml/5 tbsp freshly grated Pecorino
 or Parmesan cheese, plus extra
 to serve
sea salt and ground black pepper

This classic dish has a fascinating story that relates to the origins of the dish. The carbonari, or charcoal burners, living on the banks of rivers like the Tiber lived with just a few basics: a sheep for milk and cheese, a few hens for eggs, and a pig for fresh and cured meats. Their lives were dusted with a scattering of black charcoal flakes and the ever-present soft smoke. So the recipe honours these people, by putting together the cheese, eggs and pancetta, and the ground black pepper represents the flakes of charcoal.

Bucatini with Amatriciana Sauce
Bucatini all'Amatriciana

1 Heat the oil in a pan and fry the cubed pancetta until the fat is transparent and running freely.

2 Add the onion and chillies to the pan and fry together gently until the onion is translucent and soft. Add the tomatoes.

3 Cover and simmer for 20 minutes, stirring frequently until the sauce is thick and glossy.

4 Bring a large pan of lightly salted water to a rolling boil. Add the pasta and stir. Return to the boil and cook the pasta according to the pack instructions until al dente.

5 Drain the pasta thoroughly and return to the pan, then pour in the sauce and mix together.

6 Serve sprinkled with the cheese and a little black pepper.

Serves 4

45ml/3 tbsp extra virgin olive oil
300g/11oz pancetta, cubed
1 onion, finely chopped
½–2 dried red chillies, seeded and finely chopped
400g/14oz can chopped tomatoes
400g/14oz bucatini or other chunky dried durum wheat pasta
75g/3oz/1 cup freshly grated Pecorino or Parmesan cheese
sea salt and ground black pepper

From the little town of Amatrice, in Lazio, comes this classic sauce. It has many fans, and is one of those recipes that cause a great deal of argument and discussion among aficionados: Should the bacon be pancetta or guanciale? Is it right to use both onion and chilli? Should it not be one or the other? How much chilli, and what kind of chilli, makes this sauce just right? There are no clear answers to these questions, and the sauce remains one of those that can be tinkered with until it is exactly as you like it.

Puttanesca Pasta
La Puttanesca

1 Heat half the oil in a pan and fry the garlic with the anchovy fillets and dried chillies, until the anchovies disintegrate.

2 Add the capers and passata or tomatoes, and stir together thoroughly. Simmer for 5 minutes, then add the oregano, salt and pepper, and wine. Stir, then simmer gently for at least 15 minutes, or up to 30 minutes if you have time.

3 Meanwhile, bring a large pan of lightly salted water to a rolling boil. Add the pasta and stir. Return to the boil and cook according to the pack instructions until al dente. Drain and return to the pan.

4 Add the olives to the sauce and stir through. Pour the sauce over the pasta and add the remaining olive oil and the parsley. Toss together and serve.

Serves 4

120ml/4fl oz/½ cup extra virgin olive oil

1–3 garlic cloves, peeled and lightly crushed

3 anchovy fillets (either salted or canned in oil), rinsed and patted dry on kitchen paper

1–3 small dried red chillies, according to taste, finely chopped

25ml/1½ tbsp salted capers, rinsed, dried and chopped

300g/11oz passata/bottled strained tomatoes or canned chopped tomatoes

5ml/1 tsp dried oregano

90ml/6 tbsp dry white wine

400g/14oz penne or spaghetti

a handful of pitted black olives

30ml/2 tbsp chopped fresh flat leaf parsley

sea salt and ground black pepper

This sauce is named after the famous Roman 'ladies of the night', who are as strident, garish and obvious as the bold flavours of this sauce. The key here is that all the ingredients should sing out so that you can taste each one individually, as well as blending beautifully to create the overall taste of the sauce. It is crucial not to add the olives until the end of cooking, and not to omit the dried oregano, which is absolutely essential for the flavour.

Squid Risotto Risotto con le Seppie

Serves 4

500g/1¼lb squid, cleaned and sliced
    into rings, the tentacles cut into
    sections (see Cook's Tip)
50ml/2fl oz/¼ cup olive oil
4 garlic cloves, crushed
1 salted anchovy, boned, rinsed and
    patted dry on kitchen paper
45ml/3 tbsp tomato purée/paste
45ml/3 tbsp chopped fresh parsley
350g/12oz/1¾ cups risotto rice
½ dried red chilli, or to taste, crushed
sea salt

*This is not the black and
inky risotto of Venice, but
the strong and garlicky
version of the Lazio
coastline. Sweet-tasting
squid is a perfect backdrop
for the intense flavours that
typify the cuisine of the
region, and it appears
frequently on Lazio menus.*

1 Dry the squid on kitchen paper. Heat the olive oil in a large pan and fry the garlic and anchovy together, stirring frequently, for 3 minutes, or until the garlic is just soft.

2 Add the tomato purée and the squid. Stir everything together, then simmer for 5 minutes.

3 Add enough cold water to cover generously. Do not add salt at this stage because it will turn the squid rubbery. Cover and simmer very slowly for about 2 hours, adding more water if necessary.

4 When the squid is completely tender, add the chopped parsley and the rice. Stir and continue to cook, stirring continuously, until the rice has absorbed the water.

5 Add a ladleful of boiling water and cook, stirring, as before. Add more boiling water, a ladleful at a time, only when the liquid in the pan has been absorbed into the rice. Continue in this way until the rice is cooked – it should be tender with a little bite in the centre.

6 Stir in salt and crushed chilli pepper to taste. Transfer to a warmed platter to serve.

COOK'S TIP

Your fishmonger will prepare squid for you, but you can also do it yourself. Wash the squid carefully, rinsing off any ink. Holding the body firmly, pull away the head and tentacles. If the ink sac is still intact, remove it and discard. Pull out all the innards including the long transparent quill. Peel off and discard the thin purple skin on the body, but keep the two small side fins. Slice across the head just under the eyes, reserving the tentacles. Discard the rest of the head. Squeeze the tentacles at the head end to push out the round beak and discard. Rinse the pouch and tentacles well.

Roman Semolina Gnocchi Gnocchi alla Romana

1 Preheat the oven to 220°C/425°F/Gas 7 and grease a shallow, ovenproof dish.

2 Put the milk in a large pan and bring to the boil. Sprinkle in the semolina while whisking constantly with the other to prevent lumps forming.

3 Continue whisking until the mixture begins to thicken, then use a wooden spoon to stir constantly for about 10 minutes, or until the mixture begins to come away from the sides and the base of the pan, and forms a soft, rounded ball.

4 Remove the pan from the heat and stir in the egg yolks, half the Parmesan cheese and half the butter. Season to taste with the nutmeg, salt and ground black pepper.

5 Dampen a work surface lightly with cold water and pour out the semolina. Spread it out flat to a thickness of about 1cm/½in using a palette knife or metal spatula dipped in cold water.

6 Cut all the semolina into even circles using a 5cm/2in pastry or cookie cutter or inverted tumbler.

7 Break up the scraps of leftover semolina and arrange them in a layer over the base of the dish – this means that none will be wasted.

8 Set aside about 25g/1oz/2 tbsp of the butter for melting at the end, then cover the semolina scraps with a few dots of butter and a sprinkling of grated Parmesan cheese.

9 Arrange a layer of slightly overlapping semolina circles on top of the semolina scraps, and cover these with a sprinkling of cheese and a few dots of butter as before. Continue in this way until all of the ingredients have been used up, except for the reserved butter.

10 Melt the reserved butter and trickle it over the top. Bake in the preheated oven for 15 minutes, or until golden. Serve immediately.

Serves 6

1 litre/1¾ pints/4 cups milk
250g/9oz/1⅓ cups semolina
2 egg yolks
100g/3¾oz/scant 1¼ cups freshly grated Parmesan cheese
100g/3¾oz/scant ½ cup unsalted butter, plus extra for greasing
a pinch of freshly grated nutmeg
sea salt and ground black pepper

This is a really soothing example of ultimate Roman comfort food. Circles of cooked semolina are luxuriously coated with butter and Parmesan cheese, then baked until golden. It makes a perfect supper dish for children, as it is delicate in flavour and sustaining. Alternatively, it can be served as a simple primo when preceding a very spicy or full-flavoured main course.

Fregola with Mussels and Clams
Fregola Sarda con Cozze e Vongole

Serves 6 to 8

1kg/2¼lb mussels
1kg/2¼lb clams
3 garlic cloves, chopped
½ dried red chilli, chopped
60ml/4 tbsp chopped fresh flat
    leaf parsley
60ml/4 tbsp olive oil
1kg/2¼lb canned chopped tomatoes
250ml/8fl oz/1 cup dry white wine
1kg/2¼lb fregola
sea salt

*Fregola is made by
combining durum wheat
flour and water – sometimes
with the addition of saffron.
It is then rolled, and the little
balls of pasta are lightly
toasted, which gives it a
wonderful, nutty flavour. In
this dish it is served with
mussels and clams in a rich
tomato sauce.*

1 Keeping the mussels and clams in separate bowls, scrub them thoroughly in several changes of fresh water until the water is completely clear. Scrape off any barnacles and pull off the 'beards' from the mussels. Drain. Discard any clams or mussels that do not close tightly when tapped against a work surface.

2 In a large pan over a low heat, fry the garlic, chilli and half the parsley in the oil for 3 minutes.

3 Add the mussels and cover the pan. Cook for about 8 minutes, or until the mussels open. Remove the pan from the heat. Discard any mussels that remain closed. Remove the mussels from their shells, and strain and reserve the cooking liquid. Return the mussels and liquid to the pan.

4 Add the canned tomatoes, stir and lower the heat to simmer gently for 15 minutes.

5 Add the wine and season with salt. Cook for a further 5–10 minutes until the mussels are cooked and the liquid has reduced slightly.

6 Put the clams into a wide pan. Cover and cook them over a medium heat until they open. Discard any that remain closed. Strain the cooking liquid and add it to the pan with the mussels. Shell most of the clams, leaving a few in their shells, and add them to the pan.

7 Cook for a further 5 minutes, until the sauce is thick and glossy. Remove from the heat.

8 In another pan, boil the fregola in salted water for 8 minutes, or according to the pack instructions, then drain and add to the sauce with the remaining parsley. Stir well, then cover with a lid and leave to rest for 3 minutes before serving.

Roman Roast Lamb
Abbàcchio alla Romana

1 Wipe the meat carefully all over in case any bone shards remain, then cut into rough chunks about 7.5cm/3in square.

2 Set a wide, deep frying pan with a heavy base over a low heat. Add the oil and butter, and heat together for 5 minutes.

3 Add the kidney and meat chunks to the hot fat, browning them thoroughly all over. Season generously with salt and pepper, add the water, then lower the heat.

4 Cover and simmer for 45 minutes, occasionally adding a little water or wine and turning the meat from time to time.

5 Pound the leaves from the rosemary sprigs with the anchovies and garlic using a mortar and pestle. Stir in the vinegar and pour this mixture all over the meat. Stir thoroughly.

6 Simmer for 5 minutes, then serve immediately, with a green vegetable such as broccoli, if you like.

Serves 4

1kg/2¼lb very young, tender lamb on the bone
50ml/2fl oz/¼ cup olive oil
a knob/pat of butter
1 lamb's kidney, cubed
250ml/8fl oz/1 cup water
350ml/12fl oz/1½ cups dry white wine or water
2 x 6cm/2½in rosemary sprigs
2 large preserved, salted anchovies, or 5 canned anchovy fillets in oil, drained
4 garlic cloves, peeled
60–75ml/4–5 tbsp red wine vinegar
sea salt and ground black pepper
steamed broccoli, to serve (optional)

The unexpected ingredients of salty anchovies and sour vinegar cut the sweetness of lamb to perfection in this Roman speciality. With a hint of garlic and rosemary, it's the most delicious way to serve tender young lamb.

Veal with Sage, Prosciutto and Mozzarella
Saltimbocca alla Romana

Serves 4

8 thin veal escalopes/US scallops,
   about 115g/4oz each, trimmed
250g/9oz mozzarella
8 slices prosciutto crudo
16 fresh sage leaves
15ml/1 tbsp plain/all-purpose flour
30ml/2 tbsp unsalted butter
120ml/4fl oz/½ cup dry white wine
sea salt and ground black pepper

1 Put the escalopes between two sheets of clear film, plastic wrap or baking parchment and beat with a meat mallet or rolling pin until about 3mm/⅛in thick.

2 Cover each slice of meat with a slice of mozzarella and prosciutto, slipping a sage leaf between the meat and the mozzarella. Dredge the underneath of each saltimbocca in the flour to just coat.

3 Melt the butter in a large frying pan with the remaining sage leaves. Lay the escalopes, covered side down, in the pan to quickly seal the prosciutto to the meat with the cheese.

4 Turn and fry the other side until opaque, making sure the butter does not colour and burn. Season to taste.

5 Cover the pan and continue to cook gently for just 1–2 minutes, or until the cheese is oozing out from under the ham and the saltimbocca is cooked through. Transfer to a serving platter and keep warm.

6 Pour the wine into the pan and boil quickly, stirring and scraping the juices from the base of the pan, for 3 minutes to create the sauce. Pour over the meat and serve.

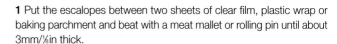

Although veal for saltimbocca is sometimes served rolled up, like a beef olive, the original recipe from Rome calls for it to be flat, with mozzarella melting on top, sealed in by a lightly fried slice of prosciutto. Fresh and fragrant sage tucked between the layers and added to the butter for frying is an essential part of the dish, as is the generous glug of dry white wine. Use Frascati, if you can get hold of it.

Roman Braised Oxtail Coda alla Vaccinara

1 Bring a large pan of water to the boil and add the chunks of oxtail and cheek. As soon as the water comes back to the boil, remove the meat using a slotted spoon. Set it aside to cool.

2 Put the chopped pork belly or bacon into a separate pan with the carrot, celery stick, onion and garlic. Fry gently together for 10 minutes, stirring frequently.

3 Add the oxtail and cheek, and brown it thoroughly all over. Season with salt and a generous pinch of crushed dried red chilli.

4 Add half the wine and cook for 1 minute to evaporate the alcohol. Pour in the diluted tomato purée and stir. Cover with a lid, and simmer for 1 hour.

5 Add the remaining wine and cook, uncovered, for 2–3 minutes to evaporate the alcohol. Cover and simmer for 3 hours more.

6 Stir in the diced celery and cook slowly for a further 30 minutes. Transfer the finished dish to a platter and serve immediately.

Serves 6

1 oxtail and 1 ox cheek, 2.5kg/5½lb total weight, cut into large chunks
200g/7oz pork belly or bacon, finely chopped
1 large carrot, very finely chopped
1 celery stick, very finely chopped, plus 5 celery sticks, diced
1 onion, very finely chopped
2 garlic cloves, very finely chopped
a large pinch of crushed dried red chilli
250ml/8fl oz/1 cup dry white wine
45ml/3 tbsp tomato purée/paste diluted in 500ml/17fl oz/generous 2 cups warm water
sea salt and ground black pepper

For thousands of years, until the Second World War, teams of oxen worked in the countryside around Rome. When they could no longer work, they were slaughtered by local workers who were paid with skins, unwanted offal and other parts of the animal – including the oxtails. This created a style of cooking that is closely associated with the Roman neighbourhood where the slaughterhouse and tanneries were located – Testaccio. Nowadays, it is a trendy area, but the traditions remain, and the local restaurants still serve these old Roman dishes, using the humblest meats.

Roman Stewed Kidneys Rognone in Umido

Serves 4 to 6

500g/1¼lb calf's kidneys, trimmed
500g/1¼lb ripe tomatoes
15ml/1 tbsp lard or white cooking fat
1 large onion, finely sliced
45ml/3 tbsp dry red wine
sea salt and ground black pepper
30ml/2 tbsp chopped fresh parsley,
   to garnish

1 Slice the kidneys and put them into a pan over a low heat. Cover with a lid and cook for 10 minutes to remove the bitter water.

2 Remove the kidneys and transfer to a sieve or strainer set over the sink. Leave to drain for at least 20 minutes.

3 Meanwhile, plunge the tomatoes into boiling water for 30 seconds, then refresh in cold water. Peel away the skins and remove the seeds. Chop them roughly.

4 In a large pan, melt the lard or fat and gently fry the onion for 10 minutes, until soft.

5 Add the tomatoes. Simmer, covered, for 15 minutes, until the tomatoes start to fall apart.

6 Add the kidneys and stir together. Add the wine and cook for 1 minute to evaporate the alcohol. Add salt and pepper and stir again.

7 Simmer for 5 minutes, then transfer to a warm serving dish and sprinkle with the parsley.

Offal is a significant aspect of Roman cuisine, particularly within the Testaccio neighbourhood, and it crops up in many different recipes. It is important to wash the kidneys carefully in several changes of cold water before using, in order to remove any trace of ammonia flavour.

Baked Eggs with Tomatoes
Uova al Tegamino con Pomodoro

Serves 4

500g/1¼lb/2½ cups canned
  tomatoes, seeded and chopped
45ml/3 tbsp olive oil
8 eggs
sea salt and ground black pepper
fresh flat leaf parsley, finely chopped,
  to garnish

1 Preheat the oven to 200°C/400°F/Gas 6. Put the tomatoes into a pan with 30ml/2 tbsp water and 2 pinches of salt. Cover and simmer slowly for 30 minutes, stirring occasionally.

2 Push the tomato sauce through a sieve or strainer using the back of a spoon.

3 Pour the oil into an ovenproof dish and pour the sauce on top of the oil. Break the eggs on top of the sauce and sprinkle with pepper.

4 Bake for 5 minutes, or until the eggs are just set but the yolks are still runny. Serve immediately, sprinkled with chopped flat leaf parsley.

This really is a delightfully simple dish. Serve it with plenty of crusty bread and a dressed green salad. If you like, you can add some chopped canned anchovy fillets or capers to the tomato sauce after straining, which will give a more robust-tasting dish.

Yellow Peppers with Capers
Peperoni in Teglia alla Napoletana

Serves 4

4 yellow bell/peppers
60ml/4 tbsp olive oil
2 garlic cloves, sliced
15ml/1 tbsp tomato purée/paste
7.5ml/1½ tsp salted capers, rinsed
    and chopped
3 anchovy fillets, preserved in oil,
    drained and chopped
sea salt

This is one of those dishes that brings together the colours, flavours and textures of the food of southern Italy absolutely perfectly. The dish is best when eaten at room temperature, with lots of green salad, bread and chilled white wine.

1 Halve the peppers and remove the seeds and membranes. Cut each pepper into four pieces.

2 Heat the oil in a pan and fry the garlic until browned. Add the peppers. Dilute the tomato purée with 45ml/3 tbsp water and pour over the peppers.

3 Season with salt, then stir. Cover and simmer for 15–25 minutes, until the peppers are soft.

4 Mix the capers and anchovies together, then stir them into the cooked peppers. Cover and leave to stand for 3 minutes before serving warm. Alternatively, serve cold.

Aubergines with Tomato and Mozzarella
Melanzane alla Parmigiana

Serves 4

3 long aubergines/eggplants, cut into
    circles
45ml/3 tbsp extra virgin olive oil, plus
    extra for greasing
250ml/8fl oz/1 cup passata/bottled
    strained tomatoes
115g/4oz mozzarella, sliced
200g/7oz Parmesan cheese, grated
15 fresh basil leaves, torn into shreds
sea salt and ground black pepper

1 Sprinkle the aubergine slices with salt and lay them in a colander. Put a plate on top and weight it down. Stand the colander in the sink for 1 hour to allow the bitter juices of the aubergines to drain away.

2 Rinse and pat the aubergine slices dry, then brush them lightly with oil. Heat the grill or broiler to high and grill or broil the aubergine slices until soft and lightly browned, turning them once.

3 Preheat the oven to 180°C/350°F/Gas 4. Put a little passata across the bottom of an ovenproof dish. Cover with a layer of aubergine slices.

4 Cover with a layer of mozzarella, a layer of passata, a sprinkling of Parmesan cheese and a few torn basil leaves.

5 Repeat the layers until the ingredients are used up, finishing with a thick layer of passata, topped with Parmesan cheese and basil. Bake for 40 minutes, or until golden. Leave to stand for 10 minutes before serving.

VARIATION
The aubergines can also be shallow fried in oil instead of grilling, and then used as above, from step 4.

Many versions of this classic recipe exist all over the south of Italy, but the principle is always the same: layers of cooked aubergine with a rich tomato sauce, basil and plenty of cheese, baked in the oven. It's a hearty dish, which tastes even better the next day.

Ring Cookies
Ciambelline

Serves 4

115g/4oz/generous ½ cup
   caster/superfine sugar
100ml/3½fl oz/scant ½ cup red wine
100ml/3½fl oz/scant ½ cup olive oil
about 250g/9oz/2¼ cups plain/all-
   purpose flour
15ml/1 tbsp lard or white cooking fat

1 In a large mixing bowl, mix the sugar, wine and oil together using a whisk. Gradually beat in the flour until you have a pliable, kneadable dough. You may not need all of the flour so just add it a little at a time.

2 Transfer the ball of dough to a bowl, cover with a cloth, and leave to rest in the refrigerator for at least 30 minutes.

3 Preheat the oven to 160°C/325°F/Gas 3 and grease a baking sheet with the lard or fat.

4 Roll the dough into 10cm/4in long sausage shapes on a floured surface. Bend them round to form rings. Arrange on a baking sheet.

5 Bake for 20 minutes, then cool on a wire rack. Serve with coffee, if you like.

Designed specifically to be dunked, these unusual ring-shaped biscuits are hard in texture so that they won't disintegrate when dipped into wine at the end of a meal. They are also delicious with frothy, milky coffee for a traditional Italian breakfast.

Easter Cake La Pastiera

1 Preheat the oven to 180°C/350°F/Gas 4 and generously grease a 30cm/12in diameter flan tin or pan with butter.

2 Put the wheat grain into a pan and add the milk, butter and grated lemon rind. Simmer slowly over a low heat for 10 minutes, or until creamy.

3 In a mixing bowl, whisk together the ricotta cheese, sugar, the 5 eggs and 2 of the egg yolks, the vanilla, orange flower water and cinnamon. Work this mixture together until smooth, and then mix in the glacé fruit and candied peel, and the creamy grain.

4 Roll out the pastry on a floured surface to 5mm/¼in thick and use to line the flan tin. Cut all the excess pastry into 1cm/½in wide, 30cm/12in long strips to make the lattice topping of your pastiera. Set aside.

5 Beat the remaining egg yolk. Pour the ricotta and grain mixture into the tart case and arrange the strips of pastry in a lattice pattern.

6 Brush the pastry with the beaten egg yolk. Bake for 1½ hours, or until golden brown. Remove from the oven and leave to cool.

7 Sprinkle the pastiera lightly with icing sugar just before serving. Once baked, the pastiera can be kept in the refrigerator for 3 days, during which time it will improve daily.

This time-honoured cake originates in the city of Naples and the surrounding region of Campania, and dates back many centuries to ancient Rome. It was traditionally made to symbolize fertility and was always baked to celebrate the beginning of spring.

Serves 8 to 12

400g/14oz cooked wheat grain
 (available from Italian
 delicatessens)
100ml/3½fl oz/scant ½ cup milk
30g/1¼oz unsalted butter, plus extra
 for greasing
grated rind of 1 lemon
675g/1½lb/3 cups ricotta cheese
600g/1lb 5oz/3 cups caster/
 superfine sugar
5 eggs, plus 3 egg yolks
10ml/2 tsp vanilla extract
15ml/1 tbsp orange flower water
a pinch of ground cinnamon
50g/2oz glacé/candied citron,
 chopped
50g/2oz candied orange peel,
 chopped
50g/2oz mixed glacé/candied
 fruit, chopped
1kg/2¼lb shortcrust pastry
plain/all-purpose flour, for dusting
icing/confectioners' sugar,
 for dusting

Civitavecchia Cake Pizza Dolce di Civitavecchia

Serves 8

50g/2oz fresh yeast

45ml/3 tbsp warm water

115g/4oz/1 cup, plus 300g/11oz/
2¾ cups, plain/all-purpose flour,
plus extra for dusting

375g/13oz cooking chocolate

7 egg yolks

150g/5oz/¾ cup caster/superfine
sugar

50g/2oz/¼ cup ricotta cheese

45ml/3 tbsp dark rum

115g/4oz/⅔ cup lard or white
cooking fat, cubed

45ml/3 tbsp sunflower oil, for
greasing

45ml/3 tbsp icing/confectioners'
sugar, sifted

*This rich yeast cake is from
Civitavecchia, a coastal
town in the province of
Rome. It is flavoured with
plenty of chocolate and a
good splash of rum. Start
preparations the day before,
as the dough will need to
rise throughout the night.*

1 Cream the yeast in the warm water and mix into the 115g/4oz/1 cup flour to make a small ball of dough. Put in a bowl and cover with a damp cloth. Leave in a warm place to rise overnight.

2 The next day, melt 250g/9oz chocolate in a heatproof bowl set over a pan of gently simmering water. Remove the bowl from the heat and set aside, but do not allow it to harden.

3 In a bowl, beat 6 of the egg yolks with the sugar, using a whisk, until pale and light. Beat in the ricotta cheese and the rum, then carefully stir in the melted chocolate using a wooden spoon.

4 Add this mixture to the bowl containing the risen ball of dough and knead together lightly to incorporate the mixture into the dough.

5 Add the remaining flour and the lard or white fat, and knead until the dough comes together.

6 Put the dough on a work surface and knead everything together very thoroughly. Transfer the dough to a bowl, cover with a damp cloth and leave to rise for 1 hour or until doubled in volume.

7 Grease a 28cm/11in cake tin or pan with the sunflower oil. Put the dough on a floured work surface. Knock back or punch down the dough, then transfer it into the prepared cake tin.

8 Place the tin in a warm place to rise for 1 hour or until the dough has risen above the top of the tin.

9 Preheat the oven to 160°C/325°F/Gas 3. Beat the remaining egg yolk and use it to brush the top of the risen dough. Dust with icing sugar and bake for 45 minutes, or until golden and firm.

10 Cool the cake in the tin, then turn out. Melt the remaining chocolate in a heatproof bowl set over a pan of gently simmering water. Drizzle over the cake and allow to harden before serving.

St Joseph's Day Choux Buns
Bignè di San Giuseppe

Makes about 24 buns

130g/4½oz/generous ½ cup
   unsalted butter
250ml/8fl oz/1 cup cold water
150g/5oz/1¼ cups plain/
   all-purpose flour
4 eggs, beaten
sunflower oil, for deep-frying
caster/superfine sugar, for dusting

1 Put the butter and water in a pan. Heat to melt the butter and then boil. Add the flour all at once and stir constantly. Cook for 2 minutes, or until the mixture pulls away from the sides of the pan, forming a ball. Remove from the heat and allow to cool. Wrap the dough in clear film or plastic wrap and chill in the refrigerator for 30 minutes.

2 Transfer the dough to a bowl. Using a wooden spoon mix the dough for 1–2 minutes. Gradually add the beaten eggs, mixing the dough until smooth each time. The dough should be soft and glossy.

3 Heat the sunflower oil in a large pan or deep-fryer until a cube of bread, dropped into the oil, sizzles instantly. Using two teaspoons, scoop balls of the mixture into the hot oil. Leave until they are puffy and golden. Remove with a slotted spoon and drain on kitchen paper. Lightly toss the cooked buns in caster sugar, and serve warm.

The story goes that St Joseph, patron saint of fathers, was a carpenter and many carpenters of that time had a sideline in selling fried street food as a way of supplementing their income, such as the famous bignè. These buns are traditionally eaten on St Joseph's Day, which is also Father's Day in Italy.

Nutritional notes

Vegetable Soup with Semolina: Energy 204kcal/854kJ; Protein 8.6g; Carbohydrate 21.3g, of which sugars 6.6g; Fat 10g, of which saturates 6.1g; Cholesterol 27mg; Calcium 190mg; Fibre 2.6g; Sodium 202mg.

Rice and Broad Bean Soup: Energy 507kcal/2111kJ; Protein 14.4g; Carbohydrate 61.3g, of which sugars 3.1g; Fat 22.7g, of which saturates 5.8g; Cholesterol 13mg; Calcium 87mg; Fibre 8.5g; Sodium 50mg.

Roman Egg and Cheese Soup: Energy 245kcal/1030kJ; Protein 14.1g; Carbohydrate 27.5g, of which sugars 1.3g; Fat 9.4g, of which saturates 4.1g; Cholesterol 110mg; Calcium 246mg; Fibre 1.1g; Sodium 424mg.

Deep-fried Mozzarella Sandwiches: Energy 428kcal/1789kJ; Protein 18.9g; Carbohydrate 30.5g, of which sugars 2.7g; Fat 26.6g, of which saturates 10.4g; Cholesterol 129mg; Calcium 331mg; Fibre 1.9g; Sodium 539mg.

Cheese Skewers with Anchovy Sauce: Energy 712kcal/2971kJ; Protein 23.2g; Carbohydrate 49.7g, of which sugars 3g; Fat 48.2g, of which saturates 31g; Cholesterol 130mg; Calcium 401mg; Fibre 1.5g; Sodium 1161mg.

Roman Cheese and Ham Fritters: Energy 436kcal/1800kJ; Protein 17g; Carbohydrate 0.2g, of which sugars 0.2g; Fat 40.2g, of which saturates 17.3g; Cholesterol 222mg; Calcium 310mg; Fibre 0g; Sodium 632mg.

Spaghetti with Oil and Garlic: Energy 505kcal/2126kJ; Protein 12.8g; Carbohydrate 76.4g, of which sugars 3.5g; Fat 18.6g, of which saturates 2.6g; Cholesterol 0mg; Calcium 27mg; Fibre 3.3g; Sodium 3mg.

Rigatoni with Tomato and Ricotta: Energy 443kcal/1867kJ; Protein 17.1g; Carbohydrate 61.7g, of which sugars 8.6g; Fat 15.9g, of which saturates 6.4g; Cholesterol 25mg; Calcium 136mg; Fibre 4.1g; Sodium 100mg.

Pasta Carbonara: Energy 620kcal/2609kJ; Protein 32g; Carbohydrate 74.1g, of which sugars 3.3g; Fat 23.9g, of which saturates 9.3g; Cholesterol 194mg; Calcium 275mg; Fibre 2.9g; Sodium 890mg.

Bucatini with Amatriciana Sauce: Energy 725kcal/3043kJ; Protein 31.9g; Carbohydrate 77.2g, of which sugars 6.4g; Fat 34.2g, of which saturates 11.5g; Cholesterol 68mg; Calcium 262mg; Fibre 3.9g; Sodium 1162mg.

Puttanesca Pasta: Energy 592kcal/2489kJ; Protein 14.5g; Carbohydrate 77g, of which sugars 6.1g; Fat 25.8g, of which saturates 3.5g; Cholesterol 0mg; Calcium 88mg; Fibre 5g; Sodium 726mg.

Squid Risotto: Energy 503kcal/2107kJ; Protein 26.8g; Carbohydrate 73.1g, of which sugars 1.7g; Fat 11.1g, of which saturates 1.7g; Cholesterol 281mg; Calcium 63mg; Fibre 0.9g; Sodium 198mg.

Roman Semolina Gnocchi: Energy 441kcal/1848kJ; Protein 17.6g; Carbohydrate 40.6g, of which sugars 8.3g; Fat 24.5g, of which saturates 14.6g; Cholesterol 132mg; Calcium 418mg; Fibre 0.9g; Sodium 406mg.

Fregola with Mussels and Clams: Energy 597kcal/2531kJ; Protein 27.7g; Carbohydrate 98.7g, of which sugars 8.35g; Fat 10.7g, of which saturates 1.6g; Cholesterol 45mg; Calcium 101mg; Fibre 5.2g; Sodium 589mg.

Roman Roast Lamb: Energy 493kcal/2057kJ; Protein 38.5g; Carbohydrate 0.7g, of which sugars 0.6g; Fat 31.4g, of which saturates 12.1g; Cholesterol 183mg; Calcium 34mg; Fibre 0.1g; Sodium 522mg.

Veal with Sage, Prosciutto and Mozzarella: Energy 540kcal/2266kJ; Protein 73.4g; Carbohydrate 3.4g, of which sugars 0.5g; Fat 24g, of which saturates 14.4g; Cholesterol 198mg; Calcium 247mg; Fibre 0.1g; Sodium 752mg.

Roman Braised Oxtail: Energy 395kcal/1646kJ; Protein 32.4g; Carbohydrate 2.8g, of which sugars 2.7g; Fat 25.4g, of which saturates 10g; Cholesterol 124mg; Calcium 39mg; Fibre 0.9g; Sodium 213mg.

Roman Stewed Kidneys: Energy 131kcal/551kJ; Protein 14.3g; Carbohydrate 6.6g, of which sugars 5.4g; Fat 5g, of which saturates 2g; Cholesterol 336mg; Calcium 27mg; Fibre 1.5g; Sodium 160mg.

Baked Eggs with Tomatoes: Energy 243kcal/1008kJ; Protein 13.4g; Carbohydrate 3.9g, of which sugars 3.9g; Fat 19.7g, of which saturates 4.4g; Cholesterol 381mg; Calcium 66mg; Fibre 1.3g; Sodium 151mg.

Yellow Peppers with Capers: Energy 168kcal/696kJ; Protein 2.9g; Carbohydrate 11.7g, of which sugars 11.2g; Fat 12.5g, of which saturates 1.7g; Cholesterol 0mg; Calcium 27mg; Fibre 2.9g; Sodium 164mg.

Aubergines with Tomato and Mozzarella: Energy 407kcal/1693kJ; Protein 26.8g; Carbohydrate 5.2g, of which sugars 5g; Fat 31.2g, of which saturates 15.6g; Cholesterol 67mg; Calcium 724mg; Fibre 3.6g; Sodium 667mg.

Ring Cookies: Energy 275kcal/1155kJ; Protein 3g; Carbohydrate 39.3g, of which sugars 15.5g; Fat 11.9g, of which saturates 2.2g; Cholesterol 1.7mg; Calcium 52mg; Fibre 0.9g; Sodium 3.1mg.

Easter Cake: Energy 809kcal/3396kJ; Protein 14.7g; Carbohydrate 110g, of which sugars 62.6g; Fat 37.6g, of which saturates 16g; Cholesterol 190mg; Calcium 144mg; Fibre 2.2g; Sodium 435mg.

Civitavecchia Cake: Energy 761kcal/3187kJ; Protein 10.3g; Carbohydrate 96.4g, of which sugars 54.3g; Fat 38.4g, of which saturates 16.3g; Cholesterol 197mg; Calcium 124mg; Fibre 1.6g; Sodium 16mg.

St Joseph's Day Choux Buns: Energy 106kcal/441kJ; Protein 1.7g; Carbohydrate 4.9g, of which sugars 0.1g; Fat 9.1g, of which saturates 3.6g; Cholesterol 44mg; Calcium 14mg; Fibre 0.2g; Sodium 53mg.

Index

Roman egg and cheese soup 20